D1378775

This Is My Story
I Come from Chile

by Valerie J. Weber

Reading consultant: Susan Nations, M.Ed., author/literacy coach/
consultant in literacy development

WEEKLY READER®
PUBLISHING

Please visit our web site at: www.garethstevens.com
For a free color catalog describing our list of high-quality books,
call 1-800-542-2595 (USA) or 1-800-387-3178 (Canada).
Our fax: 1-877-542-2596.

Library of Congress Cataloging-in-Publication Data

Weber, Valerie.
   I come from Chile / by Valerie J. Weber.
      p. cm. — (This is my story)
   Includes bibliographical references and index.
   ISBN-10: 0-8368-7234-7 — ISBN-13: 978-0-8368-7234-7 (lib. bdg.)
   ISBN-10: 0-8368-7241-X — ISBN-13: 978-0-8368-7241-5 (softcover)
   1. Chilean Americans—Social life and customs—Juvenile literature. 2. Immigrant children—
United States—Juvenile literature. 3. Immigrants—United States—Juvenile literature.
4. Santiago (Chile)—Social life and customs—Juvenile literature. 5. Chile—Social life and
customs—Juvenile literature. 6. United States—Social life and customs—Juvenile literature. I. Title.
   E184.C4W43   2007
   973'.046883—dc22   2006018402

This edition first published in 2007 by
Weekly Reader® Books
An Imprint of Gareth Stevens Publishing
1 Reader's Digest Road
Pleasantville, NY 10570-7000 USA

Art direction: Tammy West
Cover design, page layout, and maps: Charlie Dahl

Photography: All photos © Gibson Stock Photography, except page 21, courtesy of Javier's parents

Printed in the United States of America

2 3 4 5 6 7 8 9 10 09 08

Table of Contents

Cover and title page: I am learning sign language in school.

Life in Chile

My name is Javier (ha-vee-AIR). I was born in Santiago, the capital of Chile. When I was five months old, my family moved to the United States. Now we live in northern California.

Of course, I cannot remember Chile from when I was a baby. My mom and dad tell me stories of our lives there.

Chile and South America

Chile is in orange on this map.

A long, skinny country in South America, Chile lies along the Pacific Ocean. It stretches more than 2,650 miles (4,270 kilometers) from top to bottom. At its thickest, it measures less than 110 miles (180 km) wide. My dad says you are never far from the ocean in Chile.

My sister Eva was born here in the United States. She speaks in baby talk in both English and Spanish!

Sometimes **earthquakes** shake Chile. During an earthquake, the land moves. In fact, an earthquake brought my father and mother together. My dad used to live in California. When an earthquake struck Santiago, he traveled to Chile to help people. There, he met my mother. He decided to stay in Chile.

Our cat comes from Chile, too! Her name is Mori (MORE-ee). Her name is shortened from a Spanish word that means dark-skinned.

We lived in an old house with high ceilings, big windows, and a **courtyard**. It was just the three of us then — me, my mom, and my dad. We also kept a cat that we had found on the streets.

Santiago is a big, noisy city. We did not own a car there. We rode in yellow buses everywhere and sometimes took a **subway**. The subway is a train that goes underground.

From Santiago to Northern California

Six million people live in Santiago. It is a huge city with smog in the winter. My parents wanted to raise me in a small town. My dad owned a house in northern California. We moved to his house in 2001. My parents were sad to leave Chile.

Only about thirty-five hundred people live in our town.

We moved from one city near the mountains to another! The Andes Mountains run down the entire length of Chile. You can see them from almost anywhere in Santiago. We can see the Cascade Mountain range from our town in California.

The Cascade Mountains rise behind my school.

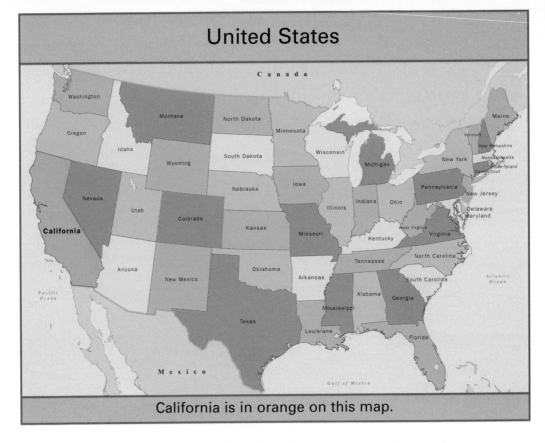

United States

California is in orange on this map.

California lies along the Pacific Ocean, too. It is a big state, with mountains, deserts, and beaches. We can ice skate here in the winter.

School Days

I like leading the class in saying the months of the year.

In school, we are learning the names of the months and days of the week in Spanish and English. Three or four kids in my class speak Spanish well. Their families talk in Spanish at home. My mother also speaks in Spanish to Eva and me at home.

My class has about sixteen kids. We are learning **sign language**.

When we lived in Chile, my mom taught in a **public school**. Classes were much bigger than my class in California. Sometimes, there were forty kids in her class! Then she worked in a small **private school**. The classes were very small.

Now, she helps in my classroom. She says there are more books and equipment here than in the classrooms in Chile.

My mom does miss one thing about the schools in Chile — the uniforms! My school in California does not require uniforms. I can wear whatever I want. In Chile, however, most children wear uniforms to school. They wear a jacket with a **symbol** of their school on the pocket. They also wear a white shirt and tie. Boys dress in dark blue pants, while girls wear dark blue skirts.

My friend and I are ready for gym class at school.

In California, I play on a team called the Sharks.

In Chile, many people love soccer. Children play soccer in the streets, parks, and anywhere else they can find. As in the United States, children can play in teams and **leagues**. Sometimes we play soccer at school.

Food and Shopping

Our main meal of the day is *almuerzo*, or lunch in Spanish.
My mother cooks some of our favorite foods. I love fish,
especially salmon. For dinner, we often eat leftovers
from lunch.

My mother cooks some of the same foods we would eat in Chile.
People do not use a lot of spices in Chile.

In the United States, most people buy food at large grocery stores. There are big stores in Santiago, too. We usually shopped for food at small stores and markets in the neighborhood, though. We went to the bakery for fresh bread everyday. I loved the little pears at the fruit and vegetable stands.

My dad says the food in Santiago is much better than what we buy here. The food is fresher because the fruit and vegetables grow near the city.

Our Bakery, Clothing, and Family

There are not a lot of stores in our town. We have to drive for an hour just to buy clothes or shoes. It is easy to get to our family's bakery, though. It is just around the corner from our house!

My dad used to work in a bakery in Santiago. When we moved here, he started his own bakery.

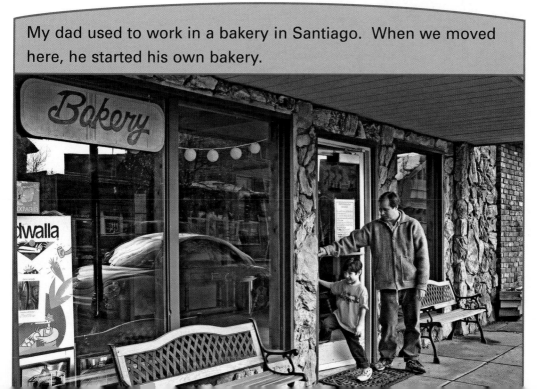

I like to help in the bakery. I wear an apron to mix the dough with my hands. They get all gooey.

I am learning to braid strips of dough. As it bakes, this dough will become a fancy, tasty bread.

I am wearing a traditional poncho and straw hat from Chile.

Most of the people in Santiago wear the same kind of clothes as people in the United States. Sometimes they wear **traditional** clothing, too.

Some of these clothes are made by hand. Others are produced in a factory.

You can see some of the traditional clothing in my family's bakery. We sell clothes made from **alpaca** wool in Chile. Soft and warm, alpaca wool lasts a long time.

Sometimes my family goes back to Chile to visit my mother's family. My grandparents live one block from the beach in a small town. I like to play with my cousins, Ignacio and Constanza. We call Ignacio "Nacho" for short. "Nacho" plays with me in the ocean, even if it's cold. We hope to visit them in Chile soon.

Here is my family in Chile. From left to right, they are my cousin Ignacio, Uncle Virgilio, Aunt Soledad, Cousin Constanza, me, Grandpa Luis, my mother Marcela, my sister Eva, and Grandma Fresia.

Glossary

alpaca — a four-legged mammal used for its fur; alpacas look like llamas.

courtyard — a flat area open to the air surrounded by a house or other building

earthquakes — sudden movements of areas of land that can last seconds or minutes

leagues — groups of sports teams that play against each other regularly

private school — a school usually paid for by the student's family or other group

public school — a school paid for by taxes from people in the surrounding area and free to students

sign language — a language that uses hand movements to communicate

subway — a train that moves through tunnels

symbol — something that stands for other objects or ideas

traditional — based on custom or an older fashion

For More Information

Books

Chile. Festivals of the World (series). Susan Roraff (Gareth Stevens)

Chile. First Reports Countries (series). Cynthia Fitterer Klingel and Robert B. Noyed (Compass Point Books)

A Pen Pal for Max. Gloria Rand (Henry Holt and Company)

Welcome to Chile. Karen Kwek (Gareth Stevens)

Web Sites

Chile
academickids.com/encyclopedia/c/ch/chile.html
A site for further research on Chile

Sanitago
www.geographia.com/chile/santiago/index.htm
Learn more about the capital city of Chile

Publisher's note to educators and parents: Our editors have carefully reviewed these Web sites to ensure that they are suitable for children. Many Web sites change frequently, however, and we cannot guarantee that a site's future contents will continue to meet our high standards of quality and educational value. Be advised that children should be closely supervised whenever they access the Internet.

Index

About the Author

Valerie Weber lives in Milwaukee, Wisconsin, with her husband and two daughters. She has been writing for children and adults for more than twenty-five years. She is grateful to both her family and friends for their support over that time. She would also like to thank the families who allowed her a glimpse of their lives for this series.